No Longer Strangers

No Longer Strangers
Ministry in a Multicultural Society

A Report to the Anglican Church of Canada
by

Romney M. Moseley

with Recommendations and a Study Guide

Anglican Book Centre
Toronto, Ontario

Anglican Book Centre
600 Jarvis Street
Toronto, Ontario M4Y 2J6
Canada

Canadian Cataloguing in Publication Data

Moseley, Romney M., 1943 – 1992
    No longer strangers: ministry in a multicultural society

ISBN 1-55126-049-2

1. Church work with minorities — Anglican Church of Canada.
I. Title.

BX5614.M67 1993   259'.0971   C93-094559-X

Contents

Part II

"Ministry in a Multicultural Society," a report for the National Program Committee of the Anglican Church of Canada (1992), was written by the late Rev. Dr. Romney M. Moseley, Project Director and Associate Professor of Divinity, Trinity College, University of Toronto. Known also as the "Moseley Report," it is available in its entirety from the Resource Centre, Anglican Church of Canada, 600 Jarvis Street, Toronto ON, M4Y 2J6.

Management Team: Eric Lugtigheid, Dr. Ben Tsang, Ivy Williams
Research Assistant: John Frame

No Longer Strangers: Ministry in a Multicultural Society is based on the Moseley Report ("Ministry in a Multicultural Society"). Part I was adapted from the text of the report, omitting a chapter entitled "Sociological Analysis," and adding new information about decisions by General Synod, to whom the Moseley Report was submitted in June 1992. The study material in Part II was not part of the Moseley Report but was prepared for this publication by Diane Engelstad.

The Rev. Dr. Romney M. Moseley died on May 31, 1992, while presiding at the eucharist at St. Michael and All Angels, Toronto. He was a gifted leader, and he will be missed by many people. He gave himself wholeheartedly to the research and writing of "Ministry in a Multicultural Society." In the process he gathered together many groups of Anglicans across Canada who shared a concern for the multicultural nature of the Church. In the resulting Moseley Report and in the people whose voices helped shape it, Romney's influence and presence will continue among us.

Foreword

About twenty years ago when I was working in a parish in Regina, the city started a multicultural celebration much like the festival I knew from my days in Winnipeg. It consisted of a series of pavilions throughout the city, sponsored by groups representing different cultural, linguistic and national heritages. In our parish we had a number of people who had emigrated from England, and many of them were active in the St. George's Society, a group for persons of English ancestry. The St. George's Society and the St. David's Society, for those of Welsh descent, both met in our parish. I knew them well, as my own ancestry is English and Welsh. I suggested to a parishioner that the St. George's Society should have a pavilion; the parish hall could be turned into a splendid English pub with food, drink and entertainment out of the English tradition. He was horrified and said that the festival was for "ethnic" groups. "We aren't ethnic," he said, "we're British!"

I welcome the publication of this report. It tells us much about attitudes in our church as they change over the years. The people of the parish in which I live are predominantly non-British in background, reflecting the reality of the Anglican Communion, where on any given Sunday most of the people in church are not of British ancestry.

In my first year as primate, Bishop Arthur Brown and a group of people from Toronto came to see me about ways our church could more consciously reflect and more explicitly acknowledge the increasingly multicultural reality of our church. This report owes much to their efforts.

As a second-generation English-Canadian, I belong to the largest ethnic group in Canada and in the Anglican Church. It is easy to delude oneself into thinking that the majority is the only group that really matters. When we succumb to that temptation, we become cultural *oppressors*. That is a hard word, but it is the way we can be perceived. Desmond Tutu always says — speaking about apartheid — that when the oppressed are freed from being oppressed, the oppressors are freed from being oppressors. I welcome the increasing recognition of cultural diversity in our church, here in Canada and elsewhere, because when others are freed from the tyranny of being a minority, I am freed from the tyranny of being a majority.

I pray that this material may help us as we strive to respond to Jesus' call to go into all the world and proclaim the Gospel in a changing society, and I commend it to the whole church, no matter what our race or ancestry.

— The Most Reverend Michael G. Peers, Primate of the Anglican Church of Canada

Part I

Introduction

...The lessons of the first council of Jerusalem and the Book of Acts of the Apostles speak to our contemporary situation. They teach us that it is God who calls people of all races, languages and cultures into a community of faith where there is neither Jew nor Greek, slave nor free, male nor female.

As a consequence of Anglican missionary enterprise and contemporary migrations to Canada, we now see Anglicanism embodied in a variety of races and cultures. But many of our sisters and brothers have experienced rejection in society at large and also within the church. These experiences reflect the wounds and sin of the world.

With penitence for our failures and in witness to our calling, we have hope in Christ to realize our vision of the transformation of our life together so that no one is a stranger, but all saints and members of the household of God.
(from Policy Statement, General Synod, 1992)

On June 25, 1992, members of the General Synod of the Anglican Church of Canada received a report entitled "No Longer Strangers: Ministry in a Multicultural Society." The document is now known as "The Moseley Report" in honour of its author, the late Dr. Romney Moseley.

The Report is the culmination of a two-year study project and one-and-a-half decades of discussion in the Church at local and national levels. In the 1970s the Diocese of Toronto undertook several studies that attempted to make sense of the rapidly changing urban scene. In 1980 three clergy, representing a coalition of ethnic minority congregations, asked the House of Bishops to carry to the national level a discussion about the Anglican Church's response to the shifting cultural mosaic.

The Church sponsored a national muliticultural symposium in 1985 and produced a video called "A Long Way to Go." A second symposium, "Called to Be Leaven," was held in 1987. Then, in 1989, General Synod commissioned the national study, and a third symposium in 1990 defined the study's parameters.

General Synod endorsed the recommendations of the Moseley Report, as well as a policy statement on multiculturalism presented by the Program Committee (see Appendix I), and commended them to national bodies, dioceses and parishes for appropriate action. General Synod requested that the Program Committee consider providing resources that would help to implement the principles of the policy statement.

The Moseley Report calls Anglicans to "embrace the Spirit of Pentecost and overcome their fear of their fellow citizens in the household of God." It challenges the Church to rejoice in the cultural richness of the worldwide Anglican Communion and cherish the links Canadian Anglicans can have with the worldwide Church through those who have immigrated here. It acknowledges that the members of the Church of Christ are "wounded healers," called to reconcile even though they are often divided among themselves.

Close to two thousand Anglicans participated in the study. The participants reflected the diversity of age groups, geographic locations, and ethnic origins found in the Anglican Church (more on methodology and demographic information in the second chapter) and thus offered a sample of the ideas, feelings, attitudes and perceptions among Anglicans on the Church's ministry in a culturally pluralistic society. The study process itself was a step in beginning to address the challenges of a multicultural church.

In many ways, the Moseley study was modelled on the "Hendry Report," a study in the late sixties of the ministry of the Anglican Church among aboriginal peoples of Canada. (See Charles E. Hendry, *Beyond Traplines*, Ryerson Press, 1969.) The Hendry Report was key to opening a discussion of aboriginal issues in the Anglican Church and initiating dialogue between aboriginal and non-aboriginal Anglicans. The report's insights continue to assist the Anglican Church in addressing the issues raised. Similarly, the seeds for addressing multicultural issues can be found in the Moseley Report.

Because of the issues already addressed in the Hendry Report, aboriginal Anglicans were involved only incidentally in the Moseley study; no attempt was made to investigate concerns related specifically to aboriginal peoples.

Using the Study

The Moseley Report is not only *about* Anglicans, but *for* Anglicans. It holds up a mirror to the Church, and can lead the Church forward toward the more welcoming, inclusive community most participants in the Moseley study agreed the gospel calls the Church to be.

This book is a summary of the Moseley Report and its recommendations, as well as a challenge to the Church for further study and action, especially at the local level where the sense of cultural diversity in community is most keenly experienced. Part Two of the book provides resources to assist in that process. "Questions for Reflection and Study" will help you to consider the findings of the Report and how it relates to your own circumstances. The set of six Bible Studies can help you grapple theologically with the issues raised by the Study.

"We, being many, are one body, because we all share in the one bread." Understanding what this means can free the Church to transcend fears that alienate, and to take risks that liberate and lead to wholeness.

About the Study

Study Methods

The "Ministry in a Multicultural Society" study employed both quantitative and qualitative methods to collect data.

Quantitative research involved the use of a questionnaire that was distributed to randomly selected congregations (using a computer program) from across Canada, and to a larger number of congregations, selected the same way, in the Diocese of Toronto. This enabled the researchers to compile statistics from the responses, and provided a sampling of perceptions and attitudes from a cross-section of the church.

Qualitative research involved conversations with Anglicans from various cultural backgrounds, through individual interviews and collective discussions in "focus groups." Through these conversations, the researchers gained deeper insight into personal experiences and feelings related to identity and participation in the church.

In both cases, the study was limited to the *perceptions* of respondents; those perceptions aren't necessarily "correct" but offer insight into what a sample of people *believe* to be true. This should be borne in mind as you read and interpret the narratives and statistical data in the next chapters.

The questionnaire was formulated in consultation with a wide variety of constituencies in the Anglican Church. The study management team also hired a professional consultant specializing in survey and market research to guide and oversee the empirical research. For the focus group research, the team consulted with an ethnographer who aided in the cultural interpretation of some of the narratives.

Before being distributed, the questionnaires were tested on members of two national committees and at least two separate groups of clergy and laity. After modifications, 2,400 questionnaires were sent out to a random selection of 240 congregations across Canada in

March 1991; another 1,900 were sent to 190 congregations in May. An additional 1,400 questionnaires were distributed within the Diocese of Toronto when additional funding from that diocese made this possible. The response rate for the total 5,700 questionnaires sent out was 33 percent, or one in three persons.

The study was not without criticism. The research was criticized for not adopting rigorous principles of market research. Dr. Moseley agreed that, in hindsight, instructions to rectors and wardens for distributing the questionnaires within parishes could have been more precise. Nonetheless, the objective of the study was not merely to gather statistics on opinions about multiculturalism but to sample the ideas, feelings, attitudes, and perceptions of the identity and ministry of the Church within the cultural mosaic. The majority of the respondents to the questionnaire were supportive of the project and pleased that the Anglican Church of Canada had chosen to take up such a crucial issue, especially during the Canadian debate on national unity.

The Participants

Respondents to the questionnaire were asked to provide information about their age, sex, marital status, ethnic background and whether they were from the clergy or laity.

Fifty-four percent of the respondents were women and 44 percent were men (2 percent did not indicate their gender). Over half — 54 percent — of the respondents were 40-64 years of age. Twenty percent were 65 and older, 20 percent were 20-39, and 2 percent were 20 or younger; 4 percent did not indicate their age. Sixty-nine percent said they were married or live with a partner (some respondents resented the fact that these options were combined). Twelve percent were single, 9 percent widowed, 4 percent divorced; 6 percent did not indicate their marital status.

Of the respondents, 10 percent indicated they were clergy and 61 percent indicated they were laypersons. The remaining 29 percent did not respond to this question, although clergy probably constituted 10 percent of the overall sample since one of every ten questionnaires was to be filled out by the rector or warden.

As would be expected, 75 percent were Canadian by birth. Another 10 percent were born in the United Kingdom, and 2 percent were born in the United States. The remaining 13 percent came from other countries; fifty-two countries of birth were listed in all, reflecting the global distribution of Anglicans.

People with Canadian citizenship constituted 94 percent. British and American citizens constituted just over 1 percent each, with other respondents indicating a wide distribution of citizenship across Asia, Africa, Australia, Europe and the Caribbean. The respondents indicated 36 principal languages (more than one could be indicated), with English, not surprisingly, being a principal language for 97 percent of the sample. French was given by 7 percent as a principal language.

The questionnaire did not attempt to define "ethnicity" in a question on "ethnic origin," leaving it to the respondents to identify for themselves. There were 56 ethnic origins indicated. Thirty-eight percent identified themselves as Anglo-Saxon; 16 percent as Anglo-Saxon/Celtic; 8 percent as Celtic. Three percent said they were Canadian; 3 percent Black African; 1.6 percent Slavic. Many of the respondents combined two or more ethnic origins in their response.

For the focus groups, specific data about the participants are not available. While some of the groups included a wide mix of cultural backgrounds, most of them were ethnically homogeneous, consisting of members of a single ethnic group, such as Japanese or Anglo-Saxon.

What the Study Revealed About the Anglican Church in Canada

Insights gained from the study about the Anglican experience can be summarized by ten key findings:

1. Most Anglicans regard multiculturalism as a positive component of Canada's identity, but there are strong criticisms of the federal government's policy on multiculturalism.

2. The present membership of the Anglican Church of Canada includes at least 56 combinations of ethnic origins and 36 principal languages.

3. Most Anglicans believe that racial discrimination is a serious problem in Canada; but they are equally divided as to the seriousness of racial prejudice in the church. The majority think the Anglican Church is more tolerant of racial and ethnic diversity than the wider society.

4. There is widespread ignorance within the Anglican Church of Canada of the church's actions and policies regarding multicultural identity and racial discrimination.

5. Many Anglicans who are not of Anglo-Saxon-Celtic origin experience coldness, alienation and marginalization within the Anglican Church, especially in the rejection of their gifts for leadership.

6. Current leadership in the Anglican Church of Canada does not reflect the cultural diversity of its membership; neither do many of the current leaders have well developed skills of cultural sensitivity.

7. The dominant liturgical practice is perceived by many Anglicans of all cultural origins as ethnocentric, performance-oriented, insensitive and dull.

8. Small, ethnic-minority congregations have survived against great odds and much official discouragement.

9. Most Anglicans are against separatism in worship for different ethnic groups. Exceptions are made for demographic factors or language.

10. Anglicans wish to move beyond the present paternalism to a church which accepts the gifts and graces of all Christians.

Questionnaire Responses

Anglican Identity and Outlook [1]

"Cultural diversity is adequately represented in the membership of the Anglican Church of Canada." (Proposition 1)
> *Agree: 44%*
> *Disagree: 24%*
> *Not Certain 30%*

"The Anglican Church of Canada should identify itself more closely with the Church of England." (Proposition 8)
> *Agree: 21%*
> *Disagree: 62%*
> *Not Certain: 15%*

"Anglicans need to think of themselves as Christians (not Anglicans) wanting to be with other Christians all over the world. We should not separate ourselves."

"Our Anglican roots lie in the English Reformation and the Book of Common Prayer which were formative of our ethos. To deny them is to deny our 'self', a formula for destruction."

"The Anglican Church of Canada should identify itself more closely with the world-wide Anglican Communion." (Proposition 9)
> *Agree: 83%*
> *Disagree: 2%*
> *Not Certain: 11%*

"The Anglican Church of Canada is more tolerant of people from a variety of races and cultures than Canadian society." (Proposition 11)

> *Agree: 53%*
> *Disagree: 15%*
> *Not Certain: 30%*

"My Anglican identity is an important influence on my attitude toward persons from other cultures." (Proposition 12)

> *Agree: 52%*
> *Disagree: 32%*
> *Not Certain: 13%*

"My Christian identity is an important influence on my attitude toward persons from other cultures." (Proposition 13)

> *Agree: 89%*
> *Disagree: 5%*
> *Not Certain: 4%*

"The Anglican Church of Canada is successfully carrying out its mission to proclaim the Gospel to all people and cultures." (Proposition 14)

> *Agree: 46%*
> *Disagree: 17%*
> *Not Certain: 15%*

"This is indeed the only mission for any church along with aid to others."

"If we are 'successful', are we not disrespecting a person's cultural heritage? Convert a Sikh into a Christian and you rob that person of his/her cultural identity!"

"With regards to Anglicanism, it is worth recalling that we form one small part of the catholic Church and that those persons who find their home within Anglicanism love it for what it is — English by birth, catholic by nature, peculiar in its liturgy, tolerant in its theological diversity and recognizably Anglican in any corner of the globe. Admittedly, we are not every person's choice, just as we have chosen not to be Baptist or Roman Catholic, etc. etc. If remaining unrepentantly Anglican ultimately leads to the death of our denomination, then so be it. We shall not be the first nor the last to travel that path, but let us then, in good conscience, go down to the dust and even at the grave make our song: Alleluia, Alleluia, Alleluia."

"A major problem the Anglican Church of Canada faces in its ministry to persons from different ethnic groups is racial prejudice."
(Proposition 15)

Agree: 31%
Disagree: 35%
Not Certain: 32%

"...the problem [of racial prejudice] exists only in the minds of a few."

"...[R]acial prejudice is rampant in the hearts of mankind and only through Christ can these barriers be broken down."

"The world-wide Anglican Communion is primarily Anglo-Saxon."
(Proposition 16)

Agree: 22%
Disagree: 45%
Not Certain: 31%

In actual fact, the majority of Anglicans in the world are not Anglo-Saxon or Celtic in ethnic origin, but this question attempted to gage the awareness of this fact.

Worship and Congregational Life

"Liturgy in the Anglican Church reflects cultural diversity." (Proposition 5)
Agree: 26%
Disagree: 42%
Not Certain: 28%

"...[T]he prayer book is a reflection of God's Word for his people and crosses all cultural barriers."

"Christian Education in the Anglican Church reflects cultural diversity." (Proposition 6)
Agree: 35%
Disagree: 26%
Not Certain: 35%

"...[T]here is no Christian Education Program for the Anglican Church of Canada. Each parish uses whatever program it feels best meets its needs. Like everything else in this world some programs are better than others."

"My local congregation is representative of the cultural diversity of the neighbourhood." (Proposition 18)
Agree: 59%
Disagree: 24%
Not Certain: 14%

Some respondents rightly pointed out that their neighbourhood was not culturally diverse since all its inhabitants were "white English speaking" of Anglo-Saxon heritage.

"We have no Sikhs, Hindus, Jews or Arabs, etc. One might ask in turn then, Are we failures? Why should we reflect cultural diversity?"

"My local church provides the following services for immigrants, refugees, and cultural minorities [respondent to indicate as appropriate]: refugee sponsorship/programmes; special cultural events; special social services for immigrants; space for ethnic groups to meet; other (specify)." (Proposition 19)

(The responses overlap since respondents were allowed to indicate more than one activity.)

Congregation involved in refugee sponsorship: 25%
Congregation provides space for ethnic groups to meet: 20%
Congregation puts on special cultural events: 13%
Congregation offers special social services for immigrants: 9%
Not certain which activities take place at local church: 55%

"The membership of my congregation is [select one]: (a) entirely Anglo-Saxon; (b) mainly Anglo-Saxon; (c) mainly non-Anglo-Saxon; (d) Other (please specify). (Proposition 22)
Entirely Anglo-Saxon: 8%
Mainly Anglo-Saxon: 78%
Half Anglo-Saxon or mainly Non-Anglo-Saxon: 8%

"...Neither Greeks nor Jews, male nor female, just sinners trying to make a go of it with a little help from God."

"Please rate [select "high," "moderate" or "low"] the participation of persons from different cultural backgrounds in these aspects of your congregation's life: (a) social events; (b) liturgy; (c) leadership." (Proposition 23)[2]
Respondents' perception of multicultural involvement in social events:
High level: 15%
Moderate level: 32%
Low level: 37%
Uncertain about level: 16%

Respondents' perception of multicultural involvement in liturgy:
High level: 13%

Moderate level: 28%
Low level: 40%
Uncertain about level: 17%

Respondents' perception of multicultural involvement in the leadership:
High level: 10%
Moderate level: 24%
Low level: 48%
Uncertain about level: 18%

"Which best describes the community in which your local church is situated?" (Proposition 25)
Town: 24%
Urban Area: 24%
Inner City: 14%
Suburban: 15.5%
Village: 11%
Rural: 7.5%
Not Certain: 4.5%

Leadership

"Cultural diversity is adequately represented in the leadership of the Anglican Church of Canada." (Proposition 2)
Agree: 27%
Disagree: 35%
Not Certain: 36%

"Clerical leadership of a congregation should reflect its dominant ethnic membership." (Proposition 3)
Agree: 34%
Disagree: 51%
Not Certain: 13%

"The Anglican Church of Canada actively seeks out persons from different ethnic groups for the ordained ministry." (Proposition 4)

Agree: 18%
Disagree: 23%
Not Certain: 57%

"Persons from non-Anglo-Saxon backgrounds hold important positions of power in my local church." (Proposition 21)

Agree: 31%
Disagree: 56%
Not Certain: 13%

Theology

"The Gospel specifically encourages cultural diversity in the Church." (Proposition 26)

Agree: 68%
Disagree: 10%
Not Certain: 16%

"Pentecost is of vital importance to the promotion of cultural diversity in the Church." (Proposition 27)

Agree: 57%
Disagree: 9%
Not Certain: 26%

"Holy Baptism is of vital importance to the promotion of cultural diversity in the Church." (Proposition 28)

Agree: 68%
Disagree: 11%
Not Certain: 15%

"The Holy Eucharist is of vital importance to the promotion of cultural diversity in the Church." (Proposition 29)
> *Agree: 70%*
> *Disagree: 10%*
> *Not Certain: 14%*

"What do you mean by Pentecost? The baptism in the Holy Spirit? Or speaking in tongues? Or the command to go out and speak the Good News to all people?"

"Baptism is a personal commitment to Christ. It is a step of faith not of culturalism."

"The Gospel is catholic, but to derive from it political or cultural models and impose them is to twist, distort, and misuse it. The New Testament contains many theologies and models for Christian communities. The only 'specific' is to repent, acknowledge God's forgiveness, be loved and love in return, then do what you will. We are one body, one bread and one faith in Christ Jesus."

Ethnic Congregations

"Congregations from different ethnic backgrounds should worship separately." (Proposition 7)
This question evoked the strongest reaction.
> *Agree: 3%*
> *Disagree: 92%*
> *Not Certain: 4%*

"...if language is a barrier, then necessity will impose separate services."

"...unless geographically unavoidable, or specifically desired, separate worship is 'nonsense.'"

"The Anglican Church of Canada should encourage persons from different cultural backgrounds to form their own congregations." (Proposition 10)

> *Agree: 8%*
> *Disagree: 82%*
> *Not Certain: 9%*

"Worship together with many cultures would be a blessing. However, within a multi-ethnic body, fellowship and prayer groups should be separate at times, for better understanding — especially where languages differ."

'In my local church, [select as many as appropriate:] (a) more than one language is used in the principal service of worship; (b) separate services in different languages are offered; (c) a non-Anglo-Saxon Anglican congregation worships separately; (d) a non-Anglican non-Anglo-Saxon congregation worships separately." (Proposition 20) (Since respondents could choose more than one answer, it is likely that the responses overlap on the question of interaction between Anglo-Saxon and non-Anglo-Saxon congregations.)

> *More than one language used in principal service: 4%*
> *Separate services using different languages offered: 3%*
> *A non-Anglo-Saxon Anglican congregation worships separately from the principal congregation: 3%*
> *A non-Anglican non-Anglo-Saxon congregation worships separately from the principal congregation: 4%*
> *No Response: 90%*

Views of Canadian Society

Given the relevance of multiculturalism to the ongoing public debates on national unity, the research team felt it was important to elicit opinions on this subject.

"Canadians are a tolerant people." (Proposition 30)

Agree: 59%
Disagree: 23%
Not Certain: 15%

"We should aim to be tolerant but it seems without Christ, this is nigh impossible. The very nature of Canada and its diversity of peoples has enabled much tolerance between ethnic groups."

"Canada's policy of two official languages is in the best interest of all Canadians." (Proposition 31)

Agree: 36%
Disagree: 44%
Not Certain: 20%

"Bilingualism could be a bonding of people but it seems it can be and is divisive."

"Most crimes in Canada are committed by non-whites." (Proposition 32)

Agree: 8%
Disagree: 61%
Not Certain: 29%

"In metro Toronto, the press has repeatedly stated it's 60/40 non-white/white. But who cares? Crime is crime."

"Racial discrimination is a serious problem in Canada." (Proposition 33)

Agree: 59%
Disagree: 22%
Not Certain: 7%

"Yes, racialism is a problem in Canada and the world over. In a way, considering the number of different races living here, perhaps there is relatively less 'racialism' here than elsewhere, where there are not so many races in one country. Our country has fallen away from 'loving our neighbours as ourselves' and we fail to witness the Good News."

"No. Here the operative word is 'serious.' To the individual who experiences discrimination of any sort, it is always serious. When Canada compares itself with any other countries such as Japan, South Africa or Brazil to name a few, Canada stands out as a shining example of tolerance."

"It is not racial discrimination that is the problem, but racial tension caused by extremists on both sides."

"All ethnic groups in Canada participate equally in society." (Proposition 34)
Agree: 12%
Disagree: 68%
Not Certain: 15%

"Increasing the number of immigrants from the 'third world' will increase the amount of crime in Canada." (Proposition 35)
Agree: 13%
Disagree: 63%
Not Certain: 22%

"Persons who come from cultures which settle differences by violence or whose ethics and morals are not formed by Common Law will run afoul of our laws. They must change their 'codes'; if not, it would be better that they not come to Canada."

"Canada is a Big Country. Lots of room to accept New Canadians. The trouble is we accept [them] without much knowledge of their culture and being aware of their difficulties and abilities. Likewise they are not adequately equipped with what Canada expects of them. They come in, accept all the social security programmes but in many cases will not accept our laws, hence crime. This is not true of all new Canadians but the news media sometimes gives a prejudiced view. We as Canadians and members of the Anglican Church in Canada and indeed the Anglican Communion must do everything we can to study and be aware of the cultural differences — so must the New Canadians do likewise. We have opened a door for them."

"Canada is a mosaic of cultures." (Proposition 36)

Agree: 85%
Disagree: 5%
Not Certain: 7%

"Yes, and like any mosaic, the pieces keep falling out. Not until you plastify [sic] the whole thing into a solid unit will it hang together for any length of time."

"Being Canadian is more important than preserving cultural distinctiveness." (Proposition 37)

Agree: 64%
Disagree: 19%
Not Certain: 14%

"Maintaining cultural identity helps all Canadians develop a strong Canadian identity." (Proposition 38)

Agree: 49%
Disagree: 28%
Not Certain: 19%

"Both are important...I know, I am an immigrant, though not from a visible minority."

"Rubbish! If one is a 'whatever' first then Canadian comes second and second never wins!"

Multiculturalism

**"The local congregation is a good place to foster multiculturalism."
(Proposition 17)**
> *Agree: 77%*
> *Disagree: 9%*
> *Not Certain: 11%*

"You make the assumption that multiculturalism is good and that all agree with it. Many, both within and without the church, would argue that multiculturalism is divisive and in the end will not only destroy Canada but the Anglican Church of Canada along with it."

"Isn't multiculturalism the give and take of getting along together as brothers and sisters? This should be the goal of the Church with Christ as its head."

At the end of the questionnaire (Proposition 39), respondents were challenged to *"Define 'Multiculturalism'."*

> *Diverse cultures existing harmoniously within one country: 28.8%*
> *A fusion of diverse cultures to form 1 Canadian culture: 9.7%*
> *People of many Races, Cultures and Beliefs: 6.1%*
> *Freedom of Worship/equal opportunity/tolerance for all races: 6.7%*
> *Tolerant/respectful of other cultures/seeking common goals: 6.0%*
> *Promotion of cultural diversity: 6.4%*
> *Retain various cultures but be Canadian first: 12.6%*
> *Political buzzword/leads to disunity/waste of money: 8.5%*
> *No Response: 28.8%*

"People who choose to live in Canada should embrace Canadian culture. Rejoicing in one's cultural heritage is healthy and to be encouraged, but this should at all times be secondary to being Canadian. Hyphenated Canadianism should not be sponsored by the Government or the Church. Official emphasis on multiculturalism and bilingualism promotes division and we need to pursue those activities which will pull this country together rather than tear it apart.

"Perhaps a better title for your research might have been 'Ministry in a Canadian Society'. The major challenge facing Canada is to heal and unite. Our Church leaders should spend more time preaching the Gospel and less time on social issues."

"The Church should, above all, be mindful of this — a Chinese Anglican Church, a Japanese Anglican Church, or a Zambian Anglican Church may be fine and proper in their respective countries. I do not think, however, it does anything for the Canadian Anglican Church if these separate churches are encouraged here. The Church, in these circumstances, will become something else and what that something else will be, I do not know. Sometimes, I think the Church forgets its mission in trying to be all things to all people. I think that it is a great mistake, for under such constraints we may find that the Anglican Church is no longer the Anglican Church but some amorphous body; even as we may find, for the same reason, Canada is no longer Canada."

One respondent addressed the issue at length and called for caution:

"Every culture is unique in the values it promotes, the behaviour it encourages and the way it deals with life's significant events or rites of passage. A multicultural society is a society that encourages or at least allows these differences among individuals and promotes understanding among different cultural groups. Given this definition is Canada a multicultural society? Not entirely. While overt discrimination is still under control, our acceptance of significant different (non-white, non Judaic-Christian) cultures is in many ways superficial — ethnic restaurants and acceptance of alternate ways of dress do not constitute cross-cultural understanding.

"There is still strong pressure for immigrants to conform vis-à-vis language, the work ethic and interpersonal behaviour. Canadians have yet to successfully deal with the French-English cultural problems that have existed in our society since its inception. Increasing problems with other cultures reflect their increasing numbers and their improved ability to speak as cohesive groups within Canada. Cross-cultural problems in our country are going to increase not decrease.

"Is multiculturalism a good idea for Canada? Although it may be a 'politically correct' idea in a liberal democratic society, I think some caution is required....Values and behaviours can change, and have changed, in a positive way due to input from other cultures. However, as Christians and Canadians, judge we must. Cultural norms that condone political violence or discrimination should not be accepted; values and behaviour that promote self-determination and self-sufficiency should be encouraged. It is our job, as Christians, to help minority groups and new Canadians achieve this self-determination without eliminating that great majority of cultural values and behaviours that enrich their lives and, in the long run, our lives.

"Promoting cultural diversity is a political process that the Anglican Church can contribute to in a meaningful way by vocally supporting cultural groups attempting to find a role in our society. I think our aboriginal peoples need the church's support to reclaim their rights in Canada. Within the church, the clergy should play a major role in promoting racial tolerance and appreciation of alternative, but productive, lifestyles. New values and behaviours must be evaluated carefully, in a way that endeavours to preserve Canada as a democratic society seen by others as a desirable place to live, work and raise a family."

Notes

[1] On any given question there was generally a percentage of respondents who did not answer; consequently, the figures noted in this section do not always add up to 100%. The questionnaire is found in Appendix II on pages 83 – 88 .

[2] Proposition 24 asked how participation could be improved. However, confusion over how to answer the question made it difficult to interpret the responses. The majority of respondents left the question unanswered.

Focus Groups

The focus groups were an opportunity for Anglicans from a variety of ethnic backgrounds to discuss the issues raised in the questionnaire and to provide the researchers with insights into the perceptions and feelings in the groups. Questions adapted from the formal questionnaire (Appendix II) provided a guide for the topics discussed by the groups, but since the discussions were free-flowing, the results cannot always be compared directly with the questionnaire responses.

Worship and Congregational Life

In the focus groups, the issue of cultural diversity in the liturgy of the Anglican Church of Canada evoked considerable debate. The majority were not satisfied with the ethnocentrism of the church's liturgy.

Participants in the focus groups said they regarded worship and liturgy as fundamental dimensions of the church's life where culture is of vital importance. However, while they saw liturgy as facilitating a common practice of worship, they cautioned that emphasizing ethnicity could promote separatism in the worship life of the Anglican Church.

On the other hand, many participants chided the Anglican Church for transmitting tradition instead of faith. They found worship services to be rigid and formal, with clergy and choir taking the key roles. They found the Book of Common Prayer and, to a lesser extent the Book of Alternative Services, to be rigid, pre-arranged responses whose repetition Sunday after Sunday is a matter of rote learning. While they acknowledged the need for a prayer book, they also desired "freedom to interact with the spirit" without fear of being isolated, rejected or otherwise characterized as going against the Anglican tradition.

Music was seen as an effective means of fostering multiculturalism in the Church; but some were displeased with the ethnocentricism and insensitivity of some ancient Anglican hymns to cultural pluralism. They viewed music in the Anglican Church as performance-oriented, the main players being the organist and choir. In contrast, they believed the music in the "evangelical" churches to be more lively, spiritually fulfilling, more appealing to youth and not culture-bound.

In identifying images and metaphors of congregational life it was not surprising that words like "belonging," "sharing," inviting," "acceptance" were juxtaposed with experiences of alienation and marginalization. On the one hand, stories were told by some people of being welcomed into the fellowship of a local congregation, and of the satisfaction of serving the church with persons from various cultural backgrounds. On the other hand, there were some strong criticisms of the local church as an uninviting place, cold like "a refrigerator." Some talked about being marginalized as visible minorities and immigrants, tolerated but not really accepted as Anglicans. Articulate men and women told of being discouraged from assuming positions of leadership in the church; for example, as lay readers or as postulants for Holy Orders. Some had been asked by clergy to "Canadianize" their English.

Some focus group participants based their expectations of the Anglican Church of Canada upon their experiences of the Anglican Church in their native countries. Interestingly, these experiences are not always of a "modern" Anglican Church but more like the Church of England in the Victorian period.

Participants said they needed the church to be more sensitive to the interpersonal and social experiences of "visible minorities." They suggested that the church could be instrumental in diminishing the fears and tensions of cultural diversity if it was more involved in the daily lives of its members.

Leadership

Focus group participants did not see the cultural diversity of the Canadian population reflected among clergy in the Anglican Church of Canada. They viewed the Anglican Church as a "white Anglo Church" and noted that "perceptions become reality." Of particular concern was the lack of role models for youth, especially for those interested in entering the ordained ministry. While most respondents did not know the process by which persons are selected for the ordained ministry, they were suspicious of the ability of clergy to take on the emotional and social concerns of a multicultural Anglican Church. They questioned whether theological schools are really preparing their students for ministry in a multicultural society, and raised questions about the "cultural sensitivity" of clergy.

> "Priests today need to be trained in social geography, human dynamics, and the dynamics of living in a multicultural world...By doing so we should begin to live in the church of today rather than the church of hundreds and thousands of years ago...The preservation of the historical tradition is not necessarily helping us today."

When asked whether the clerical leadership of a parish should reflect its majority ethnic composition as seen on a Sunday morning, participants felt that this was not a problem in their local church. However, they were concerned about ethnic representation across the Anglican Church.

> "It is not necessary for black priests to minister to black people...but it is important to have reasonable ethnic representation in the church."

Participants generally agreed on the need for ethnic diversity in the administration of the Anglican Church. They also cited the need for role models at the parish level. They weren't sure about the extent of ethnic representation at the diocesan and national levels but felt they could assume there was cultural diversity at levels beyond support staff. On the other hand, they suspected that North American-born whites occupy the senior positions of leadership.

Theology

Theological reflection on the ministry of the Anglican Church stands out as the weakest point in the focus group discussions. Few people were able to provide more than cursory responses to questions regarding the significance of Pentecost, Holy Baptism, or the Holy Eucharist to cultural diversity in the Church. Many could not say what happened at their Confirmation.

Participants felt that Christian education in the Anglican Church does not reflect the cultural diversity in the church and does not facilitate the development of "a Pentecost Church."

Judging from these discussions, theological foundations for multicultural ministry appear to be seriously lacking at the grassroots level.

Ethnic Congregations

Interviews conducted in Asian congregations in a large metropolitan area revealed considerable frustration with diocesan and national support for their ministry. Members of these congregations include survivors of internment camps and nuclear holocausts. In some cases they included three generations of Anglicans who came to Canada from Asia as Anglicans. Their narratives were often powerful testimonies of human courage and faith.

Despite problems of language and marginalization in the Anglican Church of Canada, these congregations have maintained their Anglican identity and have resisted the proselytizing of other denominations which purport to offer a more hospitable and inviting atmosphere.

A case in point was an Asian congregation whose formation was opposed by the diocesan bishop who refused to permit a non-English speaking congregation in his diocese. His successor thought otherwise and permitted the formation of this congregation. The local diocese has since entered into a companion relationship with a diocese in this congregation's native country. The congregation survives as a small enclave within the large metropolitan diocese. Denied rental space by an Anglican church in a location that is easily accessible to the majority of its members, the congregation was housed in a less accessible location in the activities building of another Anglican church. Here two separate Anglican congregations worship in adjacent buildings at different times with little or no contact with each other. They do not even use the same liturgy: the host congregation uses the Book of Alternative Services; the tenant congregation uses the liturgy of the

Episcopal Church of the United States and hymns from a popular hymnal, both of which are available in their native language. The incumbent priest of the other congregation was not even aware of the name of the priest or what time the tenant congregation held its services.

The research team visited other dual congregations where there was a more obvious sharing of ministry. In one case, a common space for worship was shared by two distinct congregations, each with its own priest. Each congregation maintained its own space in the undercroft for business and social meetings. Services were conducted in two different languages. Two separate marquees outside the church announced their presence.

In another church, two distinct congregations were pastored by the same clergy but met at different times. Services were conducted in two languages.

How the congregations deal with the problem of multiple languages challenges their ingenuity and versatility. Participants in the focus groups did not propose concrete ways to deal with linguistic problems but suggested that congregations take this on as part of their education programs.

There are clergy who are sincerely involved in promoting cultural diversity in their parishes. Some are criticized for moving the Anglican Church away from its Anglo-Saxon-Celtic origins by including hymns and songs from a variety of cultures. In one parish, the priest recommended that rooms in the new activities building be named after recent African and Latin American martyrs. This did not go over well in the parish.

Responses to both the interviews and questionnaires indicated that "ethnicity" is understood as referring to groups of other than Anglo-Saxon or Celtic origins. "Ethnic" congregations were pejoratively characterized as a result. It follows that multiculturalism is considered a policy directed towards non-Anglo-Saxon-Celtic groups. Participants in the focus groups acknowledged that there were differences among and within ethnic groups but did not like the idea that these differences were simply being tolerated. To them, the term "tolerance" was paternalistic and indicative of a church in which "ethnocentric WASP" images of God and of Jesus are normative.

Conclusions

Understanding Cultural Diversity

This project provided a medium for Anglicans to engage in serious dialogue and reflection on critical issues facing the Anglican Church and the nation. The subject of multiculturalism evoked not only carefully reasoned arguments but highly charged emotions. It brought out some of the best and worst sentiments on what it means to be a Canadian and an Anglican.

The participants in the study allow that in a culturally pluralistic nation experiences of racial discrimination are inevitable. They are aware of the reality of racial discrimination but appear to be heartened by the teachings of the gospel on the promotion of cultural diversity in the household of God and are confident that the local church is a good place to foster multiculturalism. No explicit charges of racism were levied against the Anglican Church of Canada.

The "visible minorities" in the focus groups lamented the inadequacy of cultural diversity among the clergy, in the liturgy and in Christian education, all of which contribute to the perception that ethnic minorities are of marginal significance to the life of the Anglican Church of Canada. This sense of marginalization is aggravated by the general "coldness" of interpersonal relations in Anglican churches and by the perception that expressions of worship other than the status quo are not welcome in the Anglican Church but should be left in their native countries.

Most of the participants admitted they knew little about what the national church is doing to address problems of multiculturalism or racism; clearly, better communication about national work is needed. Participants in the focus groups were genuinely surprised that the national church had undertaken this study project and were cynical about the possibility of anything other than superficial gestures of cultural diversity coming forth from the church.

The Anglican Church of Canada can play an important role in the liberation of its members from ignorance, fear, and distrust of persons who are visibly different from the majority of the membership. This is particularly crucial at the level of the local congregation where interpersonal relations create an atmosphere for people to discover more about each other and about God. In any case, the church must be prepared to work at the grassroots level at laying theological foundations for multicultural ministry.

The continuing education of clergy on matters of cultural diversity needs to be stressed along with other matters such as human rights and gender inclusiveness. The Anglican Church of Canada and its theological colleges can no longer assume that they are educating persons for an Anglo-Saxon Church. Both the curricula and the degree of cultural diversity among the faculty will need to change.

Links with the Worldwide Anglican Communion

The study indicates that most Anglicans would like closer ties with the worldwide Anglican Communion.

While only 21% of the respondents agreed that the Anglican Church in Canada should identify more closely with the Church of England, 63% agreed — with a quarter of them strongly agreeing — that the Church in Canada should identify more closely with the worldwide Anglican communion. Only 5% disagreed with the need to strengthen these links. Thus, despite the dominant Anglo-Saxon membership of the Anglican Church of Canada and its historical identity as the Church of England in Canada, most respondents seemed to prefer closer ties to the worldwide Anglican Communion over closer ties to the Church of England. This may suggest a strong ecumenical awareness and open-mindedness towards the cultural diversity of Anglicanism.

However, 52% were unaware that the worldwide Anglican communion is primarily non-Anglo-Saxon (a factor that might have some bearing on the desire for links with the worldwide communion), and at the level of the local congregation there seems to be little knowledge of the Anglican Church in the rest of the world. In light of this, it is important that the Anglican Church of Canada do more to educate local congregations on the ministry of the worldwide Anglican Communion. There is already a deliberate effort at the national level to build partnerships in mission in other parts of the Anglican Communion. In the same way, local churches could be strengthened and illumined by the vibrant and indigenous sources of Anglican faith found around the world. The 1988 Lambeth Conference, where two-thirds of the bishops came from the "third world," illustrated the growth and vitality of the Anglican Communion in these parts of the globe.

If members of the Anglican Church in Canada sincerely want to identify more with the worldwide Anglican Communion, opportunities for doing so are right at home. Cultural diversity in the membership in the church here in Canada is a microcosm of the worldwide Anglican Communion.

"Ethnic" Congregations

While the majority of participants recognized that some non-English-speaking ethnic groups might need church services in their own language, they did not support the existence of separate ethnic congregations. On the other hand, some members of non-English-speaking congregations said they wanted to preserve their ethnically distinct congregations.

Ethnic congregations are not necessarily based on language but are sometimes the result of the missionary policies of decades ago. The national church needs to give serious attention to the vital spirituality present in these congregations and to examine their relationship to the wider church.

The question of tenant congregations renting space for worship in local Anglican churches also needs to be addressed. Is it an appropriate arrangement? Is this the same as sharing costs for the maintenance of the church? At the heart of this matter is how we understand the Christian community and models of the Church.

Given the dominant monocultural identity of most of the congregations represented, it is not surprising that there is little knowledge of the needs of multicultural congregations. Most of the information about multicultural congregations came from participants in the multicultural focus groups. These persons spoke candidly of their experiences in the Anglican Church. They welcomed opportunities to share their cultural heritage with others but felt that the churches are only interested in superficial displays of their cultural heritage, through occasional multicultural dinners and performances, for example.

Perhaps the most important step for the church would be to recognize that all congregations are "ethnic," and bear the stamp of the cultures their members bring to them. For most Anglican congregations the ethnic culture is Anglo-Saxon. Acknowledging our own ethnic identity, and making room for the ethnicity of others, would move the church a long way towards accepting the gifts and graces of all Christians.

Worship and Liturgy

Liturgy is at the core of Anglicanism. It embraces the fundamental elements of Scripture, reason, and tradition. A sizable group of questionnaire respondents (42%) did not think the liturgy of the Anglican Church reflected cultural diversity, and nearly a third weren't sure. Participants in the focus groups voiced strong opinions about the need for greater cultural diversity in the liturgy. Some felt that the concern for inclusiveness in the Anglican Church seemed to be limited to matters of sexism and language. Others, however, stressed the importance of preserving the Book of Common Prayer as the norm of Anglican liturgy.

Taking into account the delicate balance of tradition and change, every effort should be made in the area of Doctrine and Worship to solicit the contributions of culturally diverse representatives of the Anglican Church. Liturgy needs to be contextual, of course, and cultural diversity in the liturgy won't be solved by the production of books, films, audio and video cassettes. On the other hand, the church does need to make some resources for contextual liturgy available. These resources should include translations of the Book of Alternative Services into the languages of the church's Asian peoples, and a new hymnal that reflects the cultural diversity of the Anglican Church of Canada.

Leadership

A significant majority of the respondents supported the proposition that the local parish is the place for cultivating a multicultural ethos. In other words, the task of transforming the ministry and mission of the Church in a multicultural society rests primarily on the local congregation. Resources at both national and diocesan levels are needed to assist with this task.

Participants in the focus groups pointed to the scarcity of cultural diversity among the clergy and lay leadership of their congregations. While they were uncertain of the process by which persons enter into ordained ministry, they were concerned that the Anglican Church seemed uninterested in providing culturally diverse role models for youth.

A related issue is the way people are prepared for vocations in lay and ordained ministries. Local congregations play a vital role in directing people into appropriate ministry. Participants in the focus groups emphasized the importance of seeing themselves represented in the leadership of the church. Those who are called to the ordained ministry need the support of local congregations. The narratives of some of the participants from "visible minorities" revealed how little support they receive for their vocational explorations from rectors and parishioners.

It is interesting that most of the questionnaire respondents (51%) felt that clerical leadership should not have to reflect the dominant ethnic membership of the local church; yet, in actuality, the leadership of most of the churches does reflect its dominant ethnic membership. Questions were raised in the study about the degree of cultural diversity among senior staff in the Anglican Church of Canada. The suggestion of appointing national staff to oversee the church's commitment to multiculturalism was also raised. The implications of such a position should first be studied carefully. The church does not have an official policy on multiculturalism that can somehow be carried out by officials. Furthermore, while there is an acceptance among Anglicans that multiculturalism is a fact of life in Canada, some perceive it to be divisive. Elevating its significance to the level of bureaucracy might be seen as harmful to the church. On the other hand, ignoring multiculturalism means ignoring its shadow side — racism — and further relegating "ethnic" congregations to the margins.

Staff on the national level need to be backed up by a clearly defined policy on multiculturalism and appropriate volunteer support at national, diocesan, and parish levels. The Anglican Church of Canada needs to show whether it is simply carrying out policies of the federal government, or has a moral, theological and biblical imperative to promote cultural diversity in the Church. Every level of authority must demonstrate its commitment to cultural diversity in order to cultivate the multicultural and multicoloured manifestations of God's love.

Recommendations for Next Steps

At the forefront of the discussion on multiculturalism stands the image of the Church as the Body of Christ with its inherent tensions of unity and disunity, strengths and weaknesses, as St. Paul describes in his letter to the church at Ephesus (Ephesians 2.11-22). Breaking down "the dividing wall of hostility," so that there are no longer "strangers and sojourners," is a pivotal issue for the Anglican Church of Canada, as it was for the early Church. In responding to the demands of ministry in a multicultural society, the Anglican Church of Canada needs to recognize itself as "the household of God" where all are "fellow citizens."

Many of the respondents to the questionnaire, the majority of whom identified their heritage as Anglo-Saxon or Anglo-Saxon-Celtic, were concerned about the preservation of order and stability within the Canadian cultural mosaic. In most of their local churches, there has been little or no change in cultural representation for the past five years. Members of the Anglican Church should open their eyes and ears to the Good News of Christ as it is proclaimed and lived out by the "strangers" who are not overseas but in our midst. Only then will fears that the Anglican Church is being "polluted" by multiculturalism be alleviated and replaced by images and metaphors of the Church as a place of hospitality and freedom.

Multiculturalism provides the Anglican Church with a unique opportunity to recover fundamental images of the Church that are relevant to the contemporary world; for example, the Church as "The People of the Way" or a "Rainbow People" — fellow pilgrims along the road of faith, sharing the Good News with other witnesses to the love of the One who identified himself as "the Way, the Truth, and the Life."

The conclusions of this study can be summarized into five key recommendations for the Anglican Church of Canada:

1. That the Anglican Church of Canada adopt a clear policy on multiculturalism and racism which is founded on moral, theological and biblical grounds.

2. That the Anglican Church of Canada encourage cultural diversity by emphasizing our connections with the wider Anglican communion and our mission within Canadian society.

3. That the Anglican Church of Canada affirm the status of ethnically distinct congregations and seek ways to encourage the sharing of their spiritual gifts with the wider church.

4. That the Anglican Church of Canada actively promote an identity which is culturally diverse and inclusive at national, diocesan and congregational levels, especially with regard to worship and leadership.

5. That appropriate resources including staff support be made available through the national program and other agencies for implementing these recommendations.

These recommendations form the basis for the Policy Statement and Principles subsequently adopted by the national Program Committee. (See Appendix I.)

Postscript

The study attempted to evoke some theological reflection on the relation of the gospel of Christ and cultural diversity. As Canada increasingly becomes a mosaic of cultures, careful attention needs to be paid not only to cultural but also to religious diversity.

The demographic data indicate that the membership of the Anglican Church of Canada is a mirror image of the old British empire. Is the theological hermeneutic of the old empire normative for the contemporary Anglican Church of Canada? Our respondents note that their Christian identity is more important than their Anglican identity. Hopefully, this indicates a move beyond denominationalism and even clericalism. It bodes well for the Anglican Church as it illumines the Church's baptismal ministry. This ministry is future-oriented, always a movement from darkness to light, from the old ways to new life in Christ. It is inherently paradoxical in that it affirms the centrality of Christ as Saviour while resisting Christocentric imperialism. It identifies disciples of Christ as wounded healers — reconcilers divided among themselves, morally obligated to love of neighbour but unable to identify who indeed is the neighbour.

Through this vortex of paradoxes and contradictions, the Anglican Church of Canada is attempting to proclaim the Good News of Christ. The degree to which it is effective depends on the willingness of its members to embrace the Spirit of Pentecost and overcome their fear of their fellow citizens in the household of God. On this subject Paul's words to the church at Ephesus are an apt recommendation for our own pilgrimage of faith.

> So he came and preached peace to you who were far off and peace to those who were near; for through him both of us have access in one Spirit to the Father. So then you are no longer strangers and aliens, you are citizens with the saints and members of the household of God, built upon the foundation of the apostles and

prophets, with Christ Jesus himself as the cornerstone. In him the whole structure is joined together and grows into a holy temple in the Lord; in whom you also are built together spiritually into a dwelling place for God.   (Ephesians 2: 17-22, New Revised Standard Version).

Part II

In endorsing the Moseley Report and adopting the Policy Statement and Principles (Appendix I), General Synod recommended that resources be made available for Anglicans at all levels of the Church to study and act on the issues. It is hoped that the questions and Bible studies in this section will provide the means to initiate discussion at the parish and diocesan levels, and inspire expressions of faith and worship that reflect the diverse gifts of all in the community.

Questions and Activities

Questions for Reflection and Study

1. A copy of the questionnaire used in the study you have read about can be found in Appendix II. Take some time to complete the questionnaire for yourself. (Permission is granted to photocopy the questionnaire for this purpose).

2. Look at your responses to propositions 1 through 17, and 26 through 38. Compare your responses to those in the study sample (pages 20 – 34). Do you find that you are generally in agreement with the majority of respondents? For which questions do you find yourself (a) in the minority? (b) in a very small minority? How do you feel about this?

3. Propositions 18 through 25 relate to the degree of cultural diversity in the local parish. Create a profile of your own congregation by compiling into paragraph form your responses to these questions. Does it reflect the cultural diversity of the neighbourhood? Are you satisfied with the degree of cultural diversity in your congregation? If so, why, and if not, why not?

4. Select 3 or 4 quotes from questionnaire respondents (pages 20 – 34), including at least one with which you agree and one with which you don't. What would you say to the writers of these comments? If you are in a discussion group, you may want to try a role play, allowing people to try different points of view and then responding to those views.

5. What is your ethnic background? What ethnic culture do you most closely identify with? What cultural traits can you identify as your own personality traits?

6. Make a list of the things you share with all Anglicans, regardless of ethnic background. Make another list of the things you value about

your particular ethnic background and would like to share with other Anglicans.

7. Make a list of all the things you can think of that can contribute to your feeling integrated as a member of a community. Would someone of *non-Anglican* background find these things in your church? Would an Anglican whose cultural or racial background differs from that of the majority find these things in your church? What might stand in the way of someone's full participation?

8. Does the term "Canadian" include all of us? Does the term "ethnic" include all of us? Or are some people "Canadian" and some people "ethnic"?

9. "What I fear most about encouraging cultural diversity in the church is _____."

Complete the above sentence by being honest about your own concerns, even if you think they are irrational. What surprises you most about your answer?

10. As in most countries, the Anglican Church was brought to Canada by British immigrants and missionaries. In what ways is the Anglican Church of Canada an "ethnic" church? What are some of the strengths, and what are some of the weaknesses of being an ethnic church?

Interestingly, while the large majority of Anglicans in Canada are of Anglo Saxon or Celtic origin, the majority of Anglicans around the world belong to other ethnic groups. What kinds of things might need to change in your own congregation to enable it to become "home" for Anglicans who immigrate here?

11. Imagine that at some point in the future, say 10 years from now, the Anglican Church of Canada reflected the cultural diversity of Canada, among the leadership, in local parishes and at a national staff level. What differences would you notice? What would be the same? What would be gained? What would be lost? Where would you fit in?

12. What biblical themes, stories and teachings would you draw on for a "theology of ministry in a multicultural society"?

13. Are there issues important to you or your group not addressed above? What are they? (Name them.) How would you like to see them addressed?

Parish Activities

1. Create an inventory of multicultural backgrounds of the members of your parish. Invite parishioners to bring forward hymns, music, rituals, customs and traditions that could be incorporated into worship, parish gatherings and educational events throughout the year.

2. Create opportunities for parishioners to tell their own stories (during the sermon time perhaps?) about their cultural background and what they value about the particular communities they are close to.

3. Develop an inventory of the cultural make-up of the neighbourhood. You may find the most recent Canada Census figures for your neighbourhood helpful. Community organizations and neighbourhood libraries can also provide information or steer you in the right direction.

For the Diocese

Many of the above questions and suggestions can be adapted for use in a diocesan setting; for example, by substituting "diocese" for "parish." In addition:

1. How are the gifts and graces of different cultures evident and encouraged in current structures?

2. How do the current structures help or hinder full participation? What changes are needed?

Bible Studies

Bible Study Introduction and Leadership Notes

The Church has always had to struggle with the ordinary implications of the radical gospel message that God welcomes all — rich and poor, women and men, Jews and Gentiles, young and old, outcasts and leaders . . . and that as the Body of Jesus Christ, the Church is called to mirror God's action. Most Anglicans participating in the Moseley study on multiculturalism in the Anglican church agreed that the local congregation was a good place to foster multicultural inclusiveness. The Bible Studies in this section are offered in the hope that reflecting on scriptural themes will help guide congregations to respond to the cultural changes in Canadian society.

There are 6 sessions in all, dealing with the call to inclusiveness and the sharing of cultural gifts from different perspectives. The most comprehensive approach would be to proceed through all of the sessions, since the themes complement and build on each other. However, if time is limited, a selection can be made according to what seems best for that group.

These studies are intended for use by any groups who would like to grapple with biblical themes that relate to issues of inclusiveness and diversity in the Church. It is not necessary for anyone in the group to have an extensive knowledge of biblical scholarship on any of the topics, since most of the themes in these studies are familiar ones to Christians. Nevertheless, the studies can be enhanced or expanded by bringing in a guest speaker who might have special insights on the scripture passages or topics.

The structure of each study is basically the same and requires only that one member of the group serve as "facilitator" for a given session, determining how to open and close with prayer, deciding when to begin and end the different parts of the session, allowing all the members of the group to participate, and helping the group to stay on track. Each member of the group should have a copy of the book, or at least of the particular study under discussion. This will enable participants to re-read introductory comments or questions if necessary and will give them a sense of where the study is heading.

The opening and closing prayers may be chosen from the "Collects and Prayers" on pages 70 – 80. These are prayers, selected from the Book of Common Prayer, the Book of Alternative Services and other liturgical resources of the Anglican Church in Canada, that acknowledge throughout the church year the inclusive nature of the gospel and our need for God's grace in living up to our calling.

The introduction to each of the sessions provides a basic orientation to the scripture passages and theme to be explored.

There is time allotted in each session for quiet reflection on the scripture passages and their relation to the theme. In most groups, there are both those who learn from grappling with issues aloud, and those who are better able to contribute once they've had a chance to consider things on their own. The structure of the sessions provides room for both.

After the reflection time, the facilitator should ensure that all participants have an opportunity to share their insights (without anyone being forced to). The time of "sharing" is not a time for debate, although questions are sometimes helpful. If a worthwhile discussion is launched, there's no point in squelching it, but you should still try to give everyone a chance to share their reflections as originally planned.

Most of the group's time will probably be spent on discussion. The suggested questions are intended to spark discussion: there are no "correct" answers. Some of the content of the discussion will likely build, if only subtly, on the time of reflection earlier. In fact, you may already have started a good discussion that you don't want to abandon, as noted above. If time doesn't permit discussing all of the questions, the facilitator could check with the group about which topic participants are most interested in discussing.

The facilitator should also monitor that the discussion works towards something positive (ask what the Bible readings have to say on the matter, for example) and does not get stuck either on "guilt" or "finger-pointing." Generally in each study, the final discussion question will help the group to focus on Christian growth in their own community.

The group is encouraged to close with prayer. Someone might want to say a prayer on behalf of the group — the facilitator may want to arrange this ahead of time; there could be an open prayer allowing participants to offer sentence prayers (someone should be designated to end the prayer time); someone could read one of the prayers on pages 70 – 80 or from another prayer collection; or you can say the Grace or the Lord's Prayer together.

Bible Study 1

The Gospel Affirms Cultural Identity

When the group has assembled, begin with one of the collects on pages 70 – 80.

Introduction (may be read aloud):

> The Gospel comes to us out of a distinctly ethnic setting. As Roland Kawano notes in his book *The Global City*, "The gospel that we listen to week by week emerges out of ethnic isolation. It does not emerge out of mainstream Jewish or Roman religion....Jesus is an ethnic person, bound to his subculture. He does not leave it. His work and his task are begun and completed within its boundaries." Jesus was bound to this ethnic culture partly by language. He read ancient Hebrew and spoke Aramaic, the regional Hebraic dialect, but it is unlikely that Jesus knew Koine, the common language of the empire.[1]

> Jesus' confinement to his own culture is a significant aspect of the Incarnation. Although the Gospel message itself wasn't to be confined to one culture, Jesus dedicated his own teaching ministry to a particular group of people at a particular time.

Reflection

Before reading the scripture passages, take 5 minutes or so to think about your own cultural identity. What is your ethnic background? How different is it from the dominant ethnic identity of present-day Canada? When did you or your ancestors immigrate to Canada (unless you are an Aboriginal Canadian)? What do you especially value about your ethnic heritage? Think of one cultural factor that has profoundly influenced how you see the world.

When there has been enough time for quiet reflection, participants may share their thoughts briefly, if they wish, with the group.

Have either or both of the two passages below read aloud. Then discuss the questions that follow.

Matthew 23:1-15

Matthew 12:1-8

Discussion

1. What information about Jesus' culture would help you understand the passage(s)? In what way does Jesus honour the culture? In what way does he critique it?

2. Make a list of 4 or 5 things in your faith and worship experience that are influenced by culture. How does our upbringing within our own culture influence how we hear and respond to the Gospel?

3. Does Jesus' identity as an ethnic Jew matter? What bearing does ethnicity have on how the church ministers in a multicultural society?

Closing Prayer

Footnotes

[1] Kawano, Roland, *The Global City: Multicultural Ministry in Urban Canada*, 1992: Wood Lake Books, pp 112– 113.

Bible Study 2

The Gospel Transcends Cultural Identity

When the group has assembled, begin with one of the collects on pages 70 – 80.

Introduction (may be read aloud):

One of the most contentious issues for the early Church was the question of whether and how Jews and Gentiles could worship together.

To fully grasp how critical an issue this was for Jewish Christians, we need to go back to Israel's exile to Babylon nearly 600 years before Christ. The distinct way of life that marked God's chosen people was threatened in exile because it was impossible to follow all the laws, such as worshipping at the Temple in Jerusalem. Three key practices — circumcision, the observance of the Sabbath and the reading of the Law — became absolutely essential as the ways to maintain the identity of God's people. Later, these customs were observed just as tenaciously in 1st century Palestine since Roman rule and the pervasiveness of Hellenistic culture created an "exile" of a different kind. The "Table Fellowship" laws of the 1st century strictly forbade Jews from eating with "unclean" persons, including anyone who was uncircumcised.

Jesus challenged these strict rules by plucking wheat and healing the sick on the Sabbath and eating with "sinners"; this was part of the reason the religious authorities wanted to kill him. Even Peter, who had spent so much time with Jesus, had to be convinced through an extraordinary dream that "God shows no partiality" (Acts 10:34) and was clearly offering salvation to the Gentiles. Even after they accepted that revelation, many Jewish Christians believed Paul was going too far by saying that circumcision for Gentiles was unnecessary. So the "elders and apostles" gathered at what is considered to be the first Church council in order to sort out the matter of circumcision and the law of Moses and their role in the Christian life; it was decided that these practices, important though they seemed, were not required (Acts 15:10,11). Trying to get Jewish and Gentile Christians to welcome one another as sisters and brothers — there is also reason to suppose that Gentile Christians looked down their noses at Jewish Christians — became a constant theme in Paul's letters to the early Church (Galatians 3:26-29; Romans 11:13-24).

The Church has not yet come to terms with the basic but radical message that "God does not show partiality." We have all found ways to put ourselves above others and claim special status with God. Thankfully, it is not the Church's decrees that determine who are part of the family, but God's decrees; and God has welcomed all.

Reflection:

Have the following passages read aloud:
> Acts 11:1-18 (Peter's dream)
> Acts 15:1-11 (Council of Jerusalem)
> Colossians 3:9-11 (Unity in Christ)

After the passages are read, take about 5-10 minutes to reflect on the passages.

1. Note any similar words or themes in the three readings.
2. How might Colossians 3:11 have been phrased from within a Canadian context?

When there has been enough time for quiet reflection, participants may share their thoughts briefly, if they wish, with the group.

Discussion:

1. The early Church had to let go of the customs passed down from Moses because they were inappropriate requirements for Gentile Christians. Are there lifestyle or cultural customs that people must adopt within your own congregation before they are accepted as sisters and brothers in Christ? List examples on a flip-chart if possible.

2. When are cultural traditions appropriate in the Church and when are they inappropriate?

3. If Paul were to visit the Church in Canada today, what might he be looking for to demonstrate that the Gospel had taken hold? ...If he were to visit your parish?

Closing Prayer

Bible Study 3

For You Were Sojourners: Multiculturalism and Hospitality

When the group has assembled, begin with one of the collects on pages 70 – 80.

Introduction (may be read aloud):

> One of the things the people of Israel were commanded to do as God's chosen people was to provide hospitality to the stranger. The refrain was repeated throughout the Law: "Love the sojourner...for you were sojourners in the land of Egypt." (See Exodus 22:21; Leviticus 19:34; Deuteronomy 10:19). In welcoming the outsider, the people remembered their own experience of being at the mercy of others. They were also invited to reflect the very nature of God, who welcomes all.

> Hospitality was one of the key themes of Jesus' ministry. He touched lepers and healed them. He welcomed children. He blessed a humble offering of bread and fish and fed a whole crowd of people who forgot their lunch. He responded to the faith of foreigners and performed miracles among them. He welcomed to Paradise the criminal on the cross next to him .

> But Jesus was not only the "host"; he was also the "stranger." He allowed himself to be welcomed into the homes of tax-collectors and prostitutes. He asked a Samaritan woman for a cup of water. He had no home of his own and thus was completely vulnerable to the hospitality of others.

> Hospitality isn't really about "giving." It is ultimately about openness to others, about the ability to receive others into our lives and to declare as meaningless the barriers that once separated us.

> Hospitality is at the very heart of the story of God's action in the world, through the chosen people of Israel and through the Incarnation.

Reflection:

Have the following two passages read aloud:
> Isaiah 56:3-8
> John 1:9-14

After the passages are read, take about 5-10 minutes to consider the passages.

1. What do these passages say about hospitality? Jot down as many ideas and connections as you can.
2. Think of a time when you were surprised by someone's hospitality. How did you feel? What surprised you about the incident?

When there has been enough time for quiet reflection, participants may share their thoughts briefly, if they wish, with the group.

Discussion:

1. Share personal experiences of hospitality as newcomers...to a neighbourhood, a church or a social group. Those in the group who have immigrated to Canada may wish to share that experience and whether they felt welcomed in the new country.

2. In John 1:9-14, who is the "host"? How is the ability to *offer* hospitality related to the ability to *receive* hospitality? Can you link this to situations that might arise in your church community?

3. How does God's act of "hospitality" have bearing on the issue of "multiculturalism" in the Church?

Closing Prayer

Bible Study 4

Disciples of all Nations: Multiculturalism and Baptism

When the group has assembled, begin with one of the collects on pages 70 – 80.

Introduction (may be read aloud):

> When Jesus ascended to heaven, he commissioned his followers to "Go...and make disciples of all nations, baptizing them in the name of the Father and of the Son and of the Holy Spirit, teaching them to observe all that I have commanded you..." (Matthew 28:19-20). Although we can't explore all the facets of baptism in one study, it is worth noting some key elements in Jesus' words: the inclusiveness ("all nations"); the inherent unity (baptized in the name of the Father, Son and Holy Spirit); and the call to discipleship ("observe all that I have commanded").

> The Book of Alternative Services notes in part: "Baptism is the sign of new life in Christ. Baptism unites Christ with his people. That union is both individual and corporate...Christians are not just individuals; they are a new humanity" (p.146).

> What links us together through all time and in all places is that God's grace comes to us all as Gift. No Christian, no matter how faithful, has ever earned the right to be called one of God's children. By the same token, all God's children are called to discipleship. Sharing with the world the new life that has been given through Christ is not an option but a sacred calling.

Reflection:

Have the following passages read aloud:
>   Ephesians 4:1-6
>   Galatians 3:26-29
>   1 Corinthians 12:14-27

After the passages are read, take about 5-10 minutes to consider the passages and write down your thoughts on the following:

1. What is important to you about your own baptism?
2. Once you are part of the Christian community, what can the church expect of you?

When there has been enough time for quiet reflection, participants may share their thoughts briefly, if they wish, with the group.

Discussion:

1. The study conducted by the late Dr. Romney Moseley found that many Anglicans of non-Anglo-Saxon-Celtic origin experienced alienation in the church; some felt that their gifts for leadership and ministry were being rejected. How do you respond to these findings in light of the passages you read?

2. Is your own church community "inclusive"? How do you know?

3. Should the Anglican Church (e.g. your congregation) try to *attract* people from different cultures? Or is it better to just be "open" to differences? How would you like your congregation to approach this matter?

Closing Prayer

Bible Study 5

By the Same Spirit: Multiculturalism and Pentecost

When the group has assembled, begin with one of the collects on pages 70 – 80.

Introduction (may be read aloud):

> Before Jesus ascended to heaven, he charged the disciples to stay in Jerusalem to wait for the baptism of the Holy Spirit (Acts 1:4). So, together with a few others, including "the women," they "devoted themselves to prayer" for ten days. The Holy Spirit came to them suddenly, dramatically and publicly, during the Jewish observance of the Feast of First Fruits. Most striking of all about the event was the surprising ability of a few common folk from Galilee to communicate in the languages of Jews and others gathered from all corners of the Roman empire. Those who saw it asked, "What does this mean?"...

Reflection:

Have the following passages read aloud:

> Acts 2:1-21
> 1 Corinthians 12:4-13

After the passages are read, take about 5-10 minutes to consider the passages and write down your thoughts on the following:

1. In each of the passages how is the Spirit "manifested"?
2. List as many examples as you can of how "unity" is expressed in the passages.

When there has been enough time for quiet reflection, participants may share their thoughts briefly, if they wish, with the group.

Discussion:

1. What is important about the first members of the Church hearing the Good News in their own language?

2. In our Canadian multicultural society, how can the Church ensure that people experience the Good News in their own "language" as they did at Pentecost?

3. The 1 Corinthians passage about "spiritual gifts" is a Pentecost lectionary reading. What direction and assistance does it offer to you in your local church community? ...to the Anglican Church in Canada as a whole?

Closing Prayer

Bible Study 6

Of Every Race and Nation: Multiculturalism and the Eucharist

When the group has assembled, begin with one of the collects on pages 70 – 80.

*Introduction (*may be read aloud):

> It is no small thing that the Church is called the "Body of Christ." Despite our demonstrated ability to create divisions, the Church's one head is Jesus Christ, and what we do as the Church, we do as Christ's presence in the world. The bread and wine of the Eucharist are "flesh and blood" signs of Jesus' presence in our lives, in the life of the Church and in the world. The Eucharist can strengthen and renew us to keep working for unity, enabling our very differences to contribute uniquely to the functioning of the whole Body.

Reflection:

Have the following passages read aloud:
>   John 17:20-26
>   Matthew 26:26-29

After the passages are read, take about 5-10 minutes to consider the passages and jot down your thoughts on the following:

1. If the Church is the Body of Christ, what does Christ's body look like?

2. In what ways do you feel linked to the Body of Christ, physically, emotionally, and spiritually, in your own neighbourhood and in other parts of the world?

When there has been enough time for quiet reflection, participants may share their thoughts briefly, if they wish, with the group.

Discussion:

1. Canada is home to members of the Body of Christ from all around the world, including the worldwide Anglican Communion. Anglicans participating in the Moseley study indicated at least 56 combinations of ethnic origins and 36 principle languages.

In your own parish, what are some practical ways to strengthen the bond we share in the Eucharist as "people of every language, race, and nation" (Eucharistic Prayer 4, Book of Alternative Services)?

2. Turn to the Principles adopted by General Synod (1992) on pages 81 – 82 . Which principles are most applicable to your parish?

Closing Prayer

Collects and Prayers

Selected from the Book of Common Prayer (BCP) and the Book of Alternative Services (BAS)

O God, who hast made of one blood all nations...for to dwell on the face of the earth, and didst send thy blessed Son Jesus Christ to preach peace to them that are afar and to them that are nigh: Grant that all peoples of the world may feel after thee and find thee; and hasten, O Lord, the fulfilment of thy promise to pour out thy Spirit upon all flesh; through the same thy Son Jesus Christ our Lord.
(Collect for Lent, BCP p.142)

O Dieu, toi qui as créé à ton image tous les peuples, nous te rendons grâce pour la merveilleuse diversité des races et des cultures du monde. Enrichis notre vie en élargissant nos cercles d'amitié et montre-nous ta présence dans ceux qui diffèrent le plus de nous, jusqu'à ce que la connaissance que nous avons de ton amour atteigne sa perfection dans l'amour que nous avons pour tes enfants. Par Jésus le Christ, notre Seigneur.
(Actions de grâce pour la diversité des cultures et des races, Le Livre de la Prière Commune, p.689)

God of all the nations of the earth,
guide us with your light.
Help us to recognize Christ as he comes to us
in [the] eucharist and in our neighbours.
May we welcome him with love,
for he is Lord now and for ever.
(Prayer after Communion, BAS p.280)

Our great Creator,
the depths of the Earth are in your hands;
the heights of the Earth are yours also.

You are our God—and we are your people.
Guide us in your love.
(The Dancing Sun: Aboriginal Lent/Easter Resource 1993, p.10)

Creator,
we sing to you a new song,
a song of gladness for your glory among the nations,
for your work among all peoples.
We rejoice in the glory of our great God and Saviour,
Jesus Christ, who came to make us a people of his own.
May the whole Earth rejoice in the truth,
that the grace of God brings salvation to all.
(The Dancing Sun: Aboriginal Advent Resource 1992, p.23)

O God, who by the leading of a star didst manifest thy only-begotten
Son to the Gentiles: Mercifully grant, that we, who know thee now
by faith, may be led onward through this earthly life, until we see the
vision of thy heavenly glory; through the same thy Son Jesus Christ,
who with thee and the Holy Ghost liveth and reigneth, one God, world
without end.
(Collect for Epiphany, BCP p.117)

Eternal God,
who by a star
led wise men to the worship of your Son.
Guide by your light the nations of the earth,
that the whole world may know your glory;
through Jesus Christ our Lord,
who lives and reigns with you and the Holy Spirit,
one God, now and for ever.
(Collect for Epiphany, BAS p.280)

Almighty and everliving God,
who fulfilled the promises of Easter
by sending us your Holy Spirit
and opening to every race and nation
the way of life eternal,

keep us in the unity of your Spirit, that every tongue may tell of your
glory;
through Jesus Christ our Lord,
who lives and reigns with you and the Holy Spirit,
one God, now and for ever.
(Pentecost Collect, BAS p.345)

Lord God of the nations,
you have revealed your will to all people
and promised us your saving help.
May we hear and do what you command,
that the darkness may be overcome
by the power of your light;
through your Son Jesus Christ our Lord,
who lives and reigns with you and the Holy Spirit,
now and for ever.
(Collect, BAS p.359)

Grant, O merciful God,
that your Church,
being gathered by your Holy Spirit into one,
may show forth your power among all peoples,
to the glory of your name;
through Jesus Christ our Lord
who lives and reigns with you and the Holy Spirit,
one God, now and for ever.
(Collect, BAS p.383)

Blessed are you, God of all the earth; you have called us out of every
people and nation to be a royal priesthood and citizens of your holy
city. May our words of praise call the world to turn to the joy of
fellowship with you, through Jesus Christ our Lord.
(Prayer following Psalm 47 in the Psalter, BAS p.765)

Creator,
you love us with a deep compassion.
Your call is to new life.
May we, believing your deep love for us,

re-build our communities in the light of that love.
(The Dancing Sun: Aboriginal Lent/Easter Resource 1993, p.16)

Accept, O Lord, our thanks and praise
for all you have done for us.
We thank you for the splendour of the whole creation,
for the beauty of this world, for the wonder of life,
and for the mystery of love.
We thank you for the blessing of family and friends
and for the loving care which surrounds us on every side.
We thank you for setting us tasks
which demand our best efforts,
and for leading us to accomplishments
which satisfy and delight us.
We thank you also for those disappointments and failures
that lead us to acknowledge our dependence on you alone.
Above all, we thank you for your Son Jesus Christ;
for the truth of his word and the example of his life;
for his steadfast obedience,
by which he overcame temptation;
for his dying, through which he overcame death;
for his rising to life again,
in which we are raised to the life of your kingdom.
Grant us the gift of your Spirit,
that we may know Christ and make him known;
and through him, at all times and in all places,
may give thanks to you in all things. Amen.
(Thanksgiving Prayer, BAS, p.129)

Creator,
in your hands are the depths of the earth,
and the height of the mountains.
The sea is yours and your hands prepared the land.
You created the heavens and the earth,
and hold everything together.
You have rescued us from darkness
and delivered us into the kingdom of your Son.
Through your Son, Christ,

we are reconciled to you in heaven and on earth,
by making peace through his death on the cross.
We praise your holy name,
giving thanks to you always
for your covenant of love.
May we extend love and mercy
to the ends of the earth,
to those who have been our enemies,
in unexpected places.
(Prayer for meditation, The Journey, p.196)

Our Lord and Creator,
we give thanks that you are a God of light,
a God who longs to heal us and bring new life.
May we walk in the light of your love.
(The Dancing Sun: Aboriginal Lent/Easter Resource 1993, p.14)

God our Father, you have created us as your people, and you sustain
us with your hand. Help us always to give you thanks, for you alone
are worthy of thanksgiving and praise and honour, now and for ever.
(Prayer following Psalm 100 in the Psalter, BAS p.838)

Creator God,
you satisfy the desire of every living thing;
you watch over all who love you,
all creatures of the earth bless your name.
You make all things new,
dwelling among us as our God.
May we love each other as you have loved us.
(Prayer for meditation, The Journey, p.119)

Creator God,
how majestic in all the earth is your name.
You have created all things,
the mountains, the fish of the seas, the birds of the air —
and in your wisdom we are created.
You shape us in your image.
We are complete in you.

Give us grace to answer the call of your voice.
May our hands be your hands on earth.
May we see the beauty of serving you in all ways.
(Prayer for meditation, The Journey, p.134)

O Dieu, toi qui nous as faits à ton image et nous as rachetés par ton propre Fils le Christ Jésus: Regarde avec compassion toute la famille humaine. Arrache de nos coeurs l'orgueil et la haine que les infectent, abats les murs qui nous séparent, réunis-nous par les liens de l'amour, et aide-nous à travers nos luttes et nos incertitudes à accomplir ton dessein sur la terre; afin que, quand il te plaira, toutes les races et toutes les nations servent en harmonie auprès de ton trône de gloire. Par Jésus le Christ, notre Seigneur.
(Prière pour la famille humaine, Le Livre de la Prière Commune, p.665)

Most gracious God, we humbly beseech thee for thy holy Catholic Church. Fill it with all truth; in all truth with all peace. Where it is corrupt, purify it; where it is in error, direct it; where any thing is amiss, reform it; where it is in want, furnish it; where it is divided and rent asunder, make it whole again; through Jesus Christ our Lord.
(Prayer for the Church Universal, BCP p.39)

O God the Father of our Lord Jesus Christ, our only Saviour, the Prince of Peace: Give us grace seriously to lay to heart the great dangers we are in by our unhappy divisions. Take away all enmity and prejudice, and whatsoever else may hinder us from godly union and concord; that as there is but one Body and one Spirit, and one hope of our calling, one Lord, one faith, one baptism, one God and Father of us all, so we may henceforth be all of one heart and of one soul, united in one holy bond of truth and peace, of faith and charity, and may with one mind and one mouth glorify thee; through Jesus Christ our Lord.
(Prayer for the Church Universal, BCP p.40)

O Dieu, Père de notre Seigneur Jésus Christ, notre unique Sauveur, le Prince de la paix: Que ta gràce nous aide à prendre conscience des dangers que nous font courir nos malheureuses divisions. Fais disparaître les préjugés, lest haines, et tout ce qui peut empêcher la concorde et l'union telles que tu les veux. Comme il n'y a qu'un seul

Corps et un seul Esprit, une seule espérance à laquelle nous sommes appelés, un seul Seigneur, une seule foi, un seul baptême, un seul Dieu et Père de tous, donne-nous de n'avoir qu'un coeur et qu'une âme et d'être unis par un même lien de vérité et de paix, de foi et de charité, pour que, d'un même coeur et d'une seule voix nous te rendions gloire. Par Jésus le Christ, notre Seigneur.
(Prière pour l'unité de l'Eglise, Le Livre de la Prière Commune, p.668)

Creator God,
your mercy calls us to reconciliation and healing.
May we look up to see
we are standing at your gates;
and at your gates everyone is welcome.
May we seek all good.
Be with us, each one, as we go to our work this week,
help us to grow in our hearts and in our minds,
sharing the gift of love you have brought in your son,
Jesus Christ our Lord.
(The Dancing Sun: Aboriginal Advent Resource 1992, p.9)

Almighty God, you have made us in your own image. Place in our hearts the love of true liberty; grant us the power to fight evil, and so guide and direct the people of this land that we may walk in the way of justice and fairness for all. We ask this through our Lord Jesus Christ.
(Book of Common Prayer [proposed], Nippon Sei Ko Kai [Anglican Church in Japan]; translation: Sonjie E. Pearson)

Almighty and everliving God,
whose Son Jesus Christ healed the sick
and restored them to wholeness of life,
look with compassion on the anguish of the world,
and by your power make whole all peoples and nations;
through Jesus Christ our Lord,
who lives and reigns with you and the Holy Spirit,
one God, now and for ever.
(Collect, BAS p.355)

Almighty God,
you call your Church to witness
that in Christ we are reconciled to you.
Help us so to proclaim the good news of your love,
that all who hear it may turn to you;
through Jesus Christ our Lord
who lives and reigns with you and the Holy Spirit,
one God, now and for ever.
(Collect, BAS p.380)

Almighty and everlasting God,
whose will it is to restore all things
in your well-beloved Son, our Lord and King,
grant that the peoples of the earth,
now divided and enslaved by sin,
may be freed and brought together
under his gentle and loving rule;
who lives and reigns with you and the Holy Spirit,
one God, now and for ever.
(Collect for the Reign of Christ, BAS p.394)

God of freedom, you brought your people out of slavery with a mighty
hand and gave them a law of love and justice. Deliver us from every
temptation to be satisfied with false imitation of your will: with talk of
peace that masks the face of war, and thanks for plenty that leaves the
poor unfed. We pray for the coming of your kingdom, founded in
Jesus Christ our Lord.
(Prayer following Psalm 135 in the Psalter, BAS p.893)

Almighty and everlasting God, by whose Spirit the whole body of the
Church is governed and sanctified: Receive our supplications and
prayers, which we offer before thee for all...in thy holy Church, that
every member of the same, in ...vocation and ministry, may truly and
godly serve thee; through our Lord and Saviour Jesus Christ.
(Collect for Good Friday, BCP p.174)

O Heavenly Father, whose blessed Son Jesus Christ did take our nature upon him, and was baptized for our sakes in the river Jordan: Mercifully grant that we being regenerate, and made thy children by adoption and grace, may also be partakers of thy Holy Spirit; through him whom thou didst send to be our Saviour and Redeemer, even the same thy Son Jesus Christ our Lord.
(Collect for the Baptism of Our Lord, BCP p.119)

God and Father of all who believe in you,
you promised Abraham
that he would become the father of all nations,
and through the death and resurrection of Christ
you fulfil that promise;
everywhere throughout the world
you increase your chosen people.
May we respond to your call by joyfully accepting
your invitation to the new life of grace.
Grant this through Christ our Lord.
(Great Vigil of Easter Prayer, BAS p.326)

Almighty and everlasting God,
in the paschal mystery you established
the new covenant of reconciliation.
Grant that all who are born again in baptism may show forth in their lives what they profess by their faith.
Grant this in the name of Jesus Christ our Lord.
(Great Vigil of Easter Prayer, BAS p.328)

Almighty God,
in our baptism you adopted us for your own.
Quicken, we pray, your Spirit within us,
that we, being renewed both in body and mind,
may worship you in sincerity and truth;
through Jesus Christ our Lord,
who lives and reigns with you and the Holy Spirit,
one God, now and for ever.
(Collect, BAS p.385)

Creator,
your love has been poured in us through others,
we learn of your love through your child.
May we rejoice in your love for us—
and grow in love for each other.
(The Dancing Sun: Aboriginal Lent/Easter Resource 1993, p.12)

God of mercy and forgiveness,
may we who share [in the eucharist]
live together in unity and peace,
in the name of Jesus Christ the Lord.
(Prayer after Communion, BAS p.291)

Gracious God, lover of all...
you make us one family in Christ your Son,
one in the sharing of his body and blood,
one in the communion of his Spirit.
Help us to grow in love for one another
and come to the full maturity of the Body of Christ.
We ask this in his name.
(Prayer after Communion, BAS p.349)

O Almighty God,
who hast built thy Church upon the foundation of the Apostles and
Prophets, Jesus Christ himself being the head corner-stone: Grant us
so to be joined together in unity of spirit by their doctrine, that we may
be made an holy temple acceptable unto thee; through Jesus Christ our
Lord.
(Collect for Saint Simon and Saint Jude, BCP p.297)

Almighty God,
by the preaching of your servant Paul
you caused the light of the gospel
to shine throughout the world.
May we who celebrate his wonderful conversion
follow him in bearing witness to your truth;
through Jesus Christ our Lord,
who lives and reigns with you and the Holy Spirit,

one God, now and for ever.
(Collect for the Conversion of Saint Paul, BAS p.400)

Creator God,
you have created everything, and it is good —
the trees, the earth, the animals,
and above all, human life.
We pray that we may protect and care for all of life,
for the earth, for the animals and plants,
and for the treasure which is ours,
in our bodies and in our spirits.
We give thanks to those who show us
what it is to live in the light of your love.
(Prayer for meditation, The Journey, p.58)

God of pilgrims, teach us to recognize your dwelling-place in the love,
generosity, and support of those with whom we share our journey, and
help us to worship you in our response to those who need our care; for
all the world is your temple and every human heart is a sign of your
presence, made known to us in Jesus Christ our Lord.
(Prayer following Psalm 84 in the Psalter, BAS p.818)

Gracious God, you have taught us in our Saviour Jesus Christ that you
are present wherever there is love, and that two or three who gather in
his name are citizens of your eternal city. Feed us with the bread of life,
that we may grow to recognize in every human heart a sign of your
presence and an opportunity to serve you. We ask this in the name of
Jesus Christ our Lord.
(Prayer following Psalm 132 in the Psalter, BAS p.890)

God who encompasses the beginning and the end, you gave to the
Chinese people the custom of going to walk on the Spring green grass
and to sweep the tombs of their ancestors. As we commemorate those
who have passed away, help us to think of the shortness of life, to seek
the true God while there is opportunity, to endeavor to do good, and
to accept salvation. We pray also that you grant your boundless love
to those who have left us.
(Prayer at Ching Ming Festival, Book of Common Prayer - Chinese, p.91)

Appendix I

General Synod Policy Statement
(Adopted June 25, 1992)

The Anglican Church of Canada, as a part of the one, holy, catholic and apostolic church with a divine commission to proclaim the gospel of God in Christ, embraces in its mission and ministry peoples of every race and culture. In faithfulness to its calling it recognizes, affirms, and celebrates the gifts and graces of persons of all cultures, and welcomes all persons into the household of God.

The lessons of the first council of Jerusalem and the Book of the Acts of the Apostles speak to our contemporary situation. They teach us that it is God who calls people of all races, languages and cultures into a community of faith where there is neither Jew nor Greek, slave nor free, male nor female.

As a consequence of Anglican missionary enterprise and contemporary migrations to Canada, we now see Anglicanism embodied in a variety of races and cultures. But many of our sisters and brothers have experienced rejection in society at large and also within the church. These experiences reflect the wounds and sin of the world.

With penitence for our failures and in witness to our calling, we have hope in Christ to realize our vision of the transformation of our life together so that no one is a stranger, but all saints and members of the household of God.

Principles

To this end this General Synod endorses the following principles:

1. That in the activities pertaining to partnership in mission:
1.1 our connections with the worldwide Anglican communion be used

to promote the multicultural nature of our church at both local and global levels

1.2 connections be made between the call to partnership with Anglicans overseas and the call to partnership with these same people when they emigrate to Canada

2. That in the activities pertaining to evangelism and social action in Canadian society:

2.1 we actively invite and welcome people from all cultures and races into our church fellowships

2.2 we encourage cross cultural learning and relationships within congregations

2.3 we address issues that divide and oppress people due to cultural misunderstanding or racism in both church and society

3. That we actively promote an identity which is culturally rich, diverse and inclusive:

3.1 by seeking ways to honour the gifts and the heritage of ethnically distinct congregations and to encourage their sharing with the wider church

3.2 by encouraging worship which is expressive in its music, words and symbols of the activity of God in many cultures

3.3 by seeking leaders, both lay and clergy, who collectively represent the cultural diversity of our church and bring gifts that will enhance the church's life

3.4 by ensuring that educational resources, continuing education programs, and educators promote sensitivity to the multicultural nature of the Anglican Church of Canada and Canadian society

3.5 by encouraging theological schools to address issues of ethnocentrism and racism

Appendix II

Questionnaire: Ministry in a Multicultural Society

Please do not write your name on the questionnaire

Age _____ Country of birth _____

Citizenship _____ Ethnic Origins _____

Male _____ Female _____

Married/Cohabit ❏ Widowed ❏ Divorced ❏ Single ❏

Principal language(s) spoken:
English ❏ French ❏ Italian ❏ Spanish ❏ Portuguese ❏ Slavic ❏
German ❏ Greek ❏ Korean ❏ Japanese ❏ Chinese ❏ Tamil ❏
Other ❏ please specify _____

Clergy ❏ Layperson ❏ Home postal code _____

We are interested in knowing more about Anglicans and the response of congregations to the challenges of cultural diversity in Canada

Please circle *the response that best answers the statement:*

SA = Strongly agree   A = Agree   NC = Not certain   D = Disagree
SD = Strongly disagree

1. Cultural diversity is adequately represented in the membership of the Anglican Church of Canada.   SA A NC D SD

2. Cultural diversity is adequately represented in the leadership of the Anglican Church of Canada.   SA A NC D SD

3. Clerical leadership of a congregation should reflect its dominant ethnic membership.   SA A NC D SD

4. The Anglican Church of Canada actively seeks out persons from different ethnic groups for the ordained ministry.   SA A NC D SD

5. Liturgy in the Anglican Church of Canada reflects cultural diversity.   SA A NC D SD

6. Christian Education in the Anglican Church reflects cultural diversity.   SA A NC D SD

7. Congregations from different ethnic backgrounds should worship separately.   SA A NC D SD

8. The Anglican Church of Canada should identify itself more closely with the Church of England.   SA A NC D SD

9. The Anglican Church of Canada should identify itself more closely with the worldwide Anglican Communion.   SA A NC D SD

10. The Anglican Church of Canada should encourage persons from different cultural backgrounds to form their own congregations.   SA A NC D SD

11. The Anglican Church of Canada is more tolerant of people from a variety of races and cultures than Canadian society.   SA A NC D SD

12. My Anglican identity is an important influence on my attitude toward persons from other cultures.   SA A NC D SD

13. My Christian identity is an important influence on my attitude toward persons from other cultures.   SA A NC D SD

14. The Anglican Church of Canada is successfully carrying out its mission to proclaim the Gospel to all people and cultures.   SA A NC D SD

15. A major problem the Anglican Church of Canada faces in its ministry to persons from different ethnic groups is racial prejudice.   SA A NC D SD

16. The worldwide Anglican Communion is primarily Anglo-Saxon.   SA A NC D SD

Please tell us some more about your local congregation

17. The local congregation is a good place to foster multiculturalism.   SA A NC D SD

18. My local congregation is representative of the cultural diversity of the neighbourhood.   SA A NC D SD

19. My local church provides the following services for immigrants, refugees, and cultural minorities:
❑ refugee sponsorship/programmes   ❑ special cultural events
❑ special social services for immigrants
❑ space for ethnic groups to meet   ❑ other (specify) _____

20. In my local church,
❑ more than one language is used in the principal service of worship.
❑ separate services in different languages are offered.
❑ a non-Anglo-Saxon Anglican congregation worships separately.
❑ a non-Anglican non-Anglo-Saxon congregation worships separately.

21. Persons from non-Anglo-Saxon backgrounds hold important positions of power in my local church.   ❑ yes   ❑ no

22. The membership of my congregation is:
❑ entirely Anglo-Saxon   ❑ mainly Anglo-Saxon
❑ mainly non-Anglo-Saxon
❑ Other (please specify) _____

23. Please rate the participation of persons from different cultural backgrounds in these aspects of your congregation's life:

	high	*moderate*	*low*
Social events	❑	❑	❑
Liturgy	❑	❑	❑
Leadership	❑	❑	❑

24. Check the appropriate box if you think participation could be improved by these or other activities:

	Social events	*Liturgy*	*Leadership*
Doing more to welcome newcomers.	❑	❑	❑
Promoting cultural diversity, for example, in the choice of readers, servers, choir-members, chalice-bearers, delegates to synod.	❑	❑	❑
Sponsoring more culturally diverse events.	❑	❑	❑
Increasing home visits.	❑	❑	❑

Other (please specify) _____

25. Which best describes the community in which your local church is situated? ❑ rural   ❑ village   ❑ town
❑ inner city (of large conurbation)   ❑ urban   ❑ suburban

We are interested in your views of the Gospel

26. The Gospel specifically encourages cultural diversity in the Church.
SA A NC D SD

27. Pentecost is of vital importance to the promotion of cultural diversity in the Church.
SA A NC D SD

28. Holy Baptism is of vital importance to the promotion of cultural diversity in the Church.
SA A NC D SD

29. The Holy Eucharist is of vital importance to the promotion of cultural diversity in the Church.
SA A NC D SD

We are also interested in your views of Canadian society

30. Canadians are tolerant people.
SA A NC D SD

31. Canada's policy of two official languages is in the best interest of all Canadians.
SA A NC D SD

32. Most crimes in Canada are committed by non-whites.
SA A NC D SD

33. Racial discrimination is a serious problem in Canada.
SA A NC D SD

34. All ethnic groups in Canada participate equally in society.
SA A NC D SD

35. Increasing the number of immigrants from the "third world" will increase the amount of crime in Canada.
SA A NC D SD

36. Canada is a mosaic of cultures.
SA A NC D SD

37. Being Canadian is more important than preserving cultural distinctiveness.
SA A NC D SD

38. Maintaining cultural identity helps all Canadians develop a strong Canadian identity.
SA A NC D SD

39. In your own words, define multiculturalism.

_____

_____

_____

The following information is to be provided by clergy or parish wardens

40. The postal code of my church is _____

41. The average household income of my congregation in relation to the provincial average is: significantly lower ❑   slightly lower ❑ about the same ❑   slightly higher ❑   significantly higher ❑

42. On an average Sunday my congregation has an adult attendance of: 0-50 ❑   50-150 ❑   150-350 ❑   over 350 ❑ (In cases where there are 2 or more congregations in the parish give figures for the congregation in which this survey has been conducted.)

43. Please indicate the ethnic/cultural groups represented in your congregation:

_____

44. In the last 5 years the cultural representation of my congregation has changed:
significantly ❑   moderately ❑   very little ❑   not at all ❑

Please use additional sheets for comments or questions.

Appendix III

A Dialogue: Learnings from the Multicultural Study
Ken Fung and Roland Kawano
(From a presentation to the 33rd General Synod of the Anglican Church of Canada, June 21, 1992)

Roland: Tell me, Ken, what seems to jump off the page for you after reading the multicultural study?

Ken: Well, Roland, it shook me up a bit; there is high controversy and more than a bit of emotion running through a number of responses and discussions. I'm not certain how to get a handle on these issues. Any ideas?

Roland: Perhaps we need to step back for a second and take a look at our larger Anglican picture — and ask some questions about our assumptions and our priorities. Maybe a metaphor can help: what if the Anglican Church of Canada were like an artichoke? If we started to peel away the leaves, how much would we have to peel off before we got to the central core? And is that sweet *core* Anglicanism? Or are all the *leaves* that we threw away Anglicanism?

Ken: That's a helpful image for understanding the comments in the study about whether our priority should be *Anglicanism* or *Christianity*. It seems that a number of folk want us to be Anglicans first because it's a way of erasing our cultural diversity. It may, in fact, have that effect, but it won't erase our accents or our colour.

But the study shows that the majority would focus on Christianity first and Anglicanism second.

Roland: True. But you, Ken, don't just represent cultural pluralism. You and others come from churches of the old British Empire, what we now call the worldwide Anglican Communion. And the Anglican Communion has, for the longest time, been the picture of cultural diversity. There's been a remarkable change from a Communion that emphasized English traditions, to a Communion whose context has become the pluralism and colour of the third world.

Ken: Yes, and perhaps our vision in Canada needs to be more connected to all the richness of the Anglican Communion. The study shows that the real strength of the Anglican Communion is not found in North America or England, but in the third world — Africa, Asia-Pacific, the Caribbean and Latin America.

Roland: The old Empire that once covered the globe is now being re-formed in our major urban centres — more quickly than most of us realize. The demographic projections tell us that this re-formation is remaking the face of urban Canada. That means our traditional church structures are facing some real challenges. Up until now the Anglican Church has assumed that its parish, diocesan, and national structures are adequate to deal with these major changes. Romney's study is certainly saying that the church needs to reposition itself and do some serious revisioning to take advantage of all the massive changes around us.

But the study also shows there's a lot of resistance to repositioning ourselves.

Ken: One of the issues that generated a lot of resistance and emotion is the idea of developing more than one single model of church development to respond to the changes in church and society. You see, the study raises the issue of ethnic minority congregations and their viability. Many people seem to feel that *if* we have to have minority ethnic congregations, they should serve as an *interim step* towards ethnic people joining the local parish, with "ethnic" congregations eventually disappearing.

Roland: Ethnic congregations are based on what missiologists call the homogeneous model; that is, a congregation whose members have similar traditions, language, and culture. These congregations don't have cultural diversity; they are monocultural.

Ken: I've just had a remarkable insight. I am a pastor of a congregation of Chinese Anglicans, and our congregation fits the homogeneous model. But I can think of many other congregations that fit the homogeneous model. Rural parishes are a homogeneous community; so are native parishes; so are urban congregations who aren't able or willing to relate to their surroundings. And perhaps some Anglo-Catholic and Evangelical congregations are more ethnic than my congregation. Perhaps, Anglo-ethnicity, or Anglo-Celtic ethnicity is the model of all models. The homogeneous model of church development wasn't invented by ethnic minority congregations, but just taken over by us. We learned it from the larger church.

Roland: The terminology used by one of our partner churches might be helpful to us. For instance, the Italian parish in my neighbourhood, and the Chinese parish downtown, are termed "national" (as opposed to "ethnic") parishes because the language, culture, and the liturgy, etc. come from a partner, national, church. The terminology should be very helpful to us in making connections from the local and regional church to our larger Anglican Communion. The Anglican Communion has come home to our shores, and we certainly need help to make the connections between the national church, ethnic parishes, and the larger communion.

Roland: The world is changing before our very eyes. And isn't that the real conundrum? We don't all necessarily see these changes in the same way; and those who *don't want* the world to change often have a hard time seeing these changes and their full implications. I guess to help us understand the changes, we need to connect the changes in our local contexts with the changes in the worldwide communion.

Ken: Roland, aren't you going a bit too fast? The Canadian Church wishes to welcome new peoples into the church but these peoples will first have to learn the meaning of "becoming Canadian."

Roland: ...And what does "becoming Canadian" mean — is it equivalent to becoming "anglicized"? Do we have to become anglicized to be an Anglican in Canada?

Ken: No. Romney's study indicated that there are 56 ethnic origins and 36 languages within the Anglican Church of Canada, and none of these is less Canadian than the others. My point is that we need to redefine "Canadian." And my question is: does the term "Canadian" include all of us? Or are some of us "Canadian" and some of us "ethnic"? Romney's study spent a good deal of time on these issues. Romney's study recognizes that the Anglican Church of Canada is composed of diverse cultures and is itself one facet of a worldwide communion. We need to help our Canadian Church make those connections and we need a language that shows forth and models these connections.

Roland: It sounds as if you're proposing some new models for evangelism. What are you thinking?

Ken: Well, our Anglican Church is in the Decade of Evangelism. If we were simply evangelizing our culture the way we did at the turn of the century, we would probably continue without much change. But living in a time when we've witnessed the fall of the Berlin Wall and the riots in Los Angeles, and anticipate the changes for Hong Kong in 1997, we need to communicate with newcomers, as well as with the older people, using language and models that make sense.

Roland: That's an awful lot of change to expect a church to gear up for. Aren't you expecting a bit much? Aren't you asking for the face of the Anglican Church to change? How much change are we looking at?

Ken: I guess the question is: does the Anglican Church of Canada wish to continue to look and feel like the Church of British North America, like a ghetto in urban North America?

Roland: Perhaps the question should be: will the Anglican Church of Canada have the flexibility to identify with the changes and transitions all around it? When we face these changes and become identified with them, the Anglican Church and Canada and the Anglican Communion become our home.

Ken: But Roland, the Anglican Church is already my home. It was my home where I came from, and it is my home here.

But I think I can appreciate the real fear in the larger church about the challenges that come from all these changes.

Roland: It makes me think about how the ancient Chinese understood crises. They saw a crisis as made up of two parts, two characters: fear and opportunity. Romney's study has raised a lot of fear. We know what this fear looks and feels like.

But you and I have been speaking about how all these changes represent opportunities for the new cultural diversity of Canada. How can we help the larger Church see these changes and transitions as opportunities? And what is the vision and opportunity for the Anglican Church of Canada at this time? These are the kinds of questions we need to address.

Other Books on Ministry

The Ministry of the Laity
Sharing the Leadership, Sharing the Task
by Donald Peel
ISBN 0-921846-06-1 paper 158 pages

The Ministry of Listening
Team Visiting in Hospital and Home
by Donald Peel
ISBN 0-919030-57-2 paper 123 pages

The Gift of Courage
Coping with Pain and Suffering
by James Wilkes
ISBN 0-664-24394-0 paper 107 pages

Treasures of Darkness
Struggling with Separation and Divorce in the Church
by Anne Tanner
ISBN 0-921846-22-3 paper 192 pages

Caring for the Dying
A Guide for Caregivers in Home and Hospital
by Beverly Hall
ISBN 0-919891-87-X paper 80 pages

Dying, Yet We Live
Our Response to the Spiritual Needs of the Dying
by Paul Chidwick
ISBN 0-919891-91-8 paper 109 pages

Total Health
The Fourth Dimension
by George Birtch
ISBN 0-921846-34-7 paper 103 pages

Anglican Book Centre, 600 Jarvis Street, Toronto, Ontario M4Y 2J6